ABBA
GOLD

GREATEST HITS

ISBN: 978-1-84772-895-1

HAL•LEONARD®

For all works contained herein:
Unauthorized copying, arranging, adapting, recording, Internet posting, public performance,
or other distribution of the music in this publication is an infringement of copyright.
Infringers are liable under the law.

Visit Hal Leonard Online at
www.halleonard.com

World headquarters, contact:
Hal Leonard
7777 West Bluemound Road
Milwaukee, WI 53213
Email: info@halleonard.com

In Europe, contact:
Hal Leonard Europe Limited
1 Red Place
London, W1K 6PL
Email: info@halleonardeurope.com

In Australia, contact:
Hal Leonard Australia Pty. Ltd.
4 Lentara Court
Cheltenham, Victoria, 3192 Australia
Email: info@halleonard.com.au

Dancing Queen 8
Knowing Me, Knowing You 12
Take A Chance On Me 15
Mamma Mia 18
Lay All Your Love On Me 22
Super Trouper 26
I Have A Dream 30
The Winner Takes It All 34
Money, Money, Money 39
S.O.S. 42
Chiquitita 46
Fernando 50
Voulez-Vous 76
Gimme! Gimme! Gimme! (A Man After Midnight) 54
Does Your Mother Know 58
One Of Us 62
The Name Of The Game 64
Thank You For The Music 68
Waterloo 72

ABBA
A GOLDEN LEGACY

Abba Gold is one of the best-selling albums in the history of popular music, the jewel in the crown of Abba's diamond-encrusted catalogue. Originally released in 1992, it brings together 19 of the group's classic hits and is one of those rare collections that returns to the best-selling lists on a regular basis as new fans discover Abba, most recently as a result of the smash hit musical *Mamma Mia!* and the accompanying film that was released in 2008.

Time does not diminish Abba. While the four individuals that made up the group long ago decided to cease collective endeavours, the music they made together transcends eras and fashion, and has now become a solid gold template for new generations that seek to create pop music at its highest level. 'Dancing Queen' is probably the greatest party anthem ever recorded, while 'The Winner Takes It All' is regularly cited as the supreme melodic statement about broken relationships.

These two songs were released during Abba's golden era, which extended from the mid-'70s to early '80s, but it had taken the four musicians more than a decade to reach this level of finesse. In their home country of Sweden, the individual members of the group had embarked on separate careers during the '60s, coming together in 1972 under the patronage of Polar Music, a Stockholm-based record label and music publishing company run by Swedish impresario Stig Anderson.

Until this time guitarist Björn Ulvaeus was part of the folk group The Hootenanny Singers, while keyboard player Benny Andersson was a member of the pop group The Hep Stars. Both were among Sweden's top acts at the time, and when Björn first met Benny in June 1966 they developed a close friendship that would eventually grow into an outstanding songwriting partnership. By the end of the decade, The Hep Stars had split up and The Hootenanny Singers were more or less a studio act at Polar Music. In the summer of 1971, Stig Anderson offered Björn the job of house producer, and Björn insisted that Benny be hired as well.

Two years earlier, in 1969, Björn and Benny both happened to strike up romantic relationships with singers. Benny met and fell for Norwegian-born Anni-Frid Lyngstad, also known as Frida, while a romance blossomed between Björn and Agnetha Fältskog. Both girls were former dance band singers who had launched solo careers. By the spring of 1970, both couples were engaged.

There was a good deal of experimenting in the studio before Abba was born. Björn and Benny recorded together and wrote songs for others, while Frida and Agnetha continued their domestic solo careers with mixed fortunes as well as performing back-up duties in the studio. Björn and Benny's real ambition was to record English-language songs that would reach beyond Sweden, and in this regard Stig Anderson, whose ambition was matched only by his diligence, was unusually supportive.

Björn and Benny were well aware of their own shortcomings as singers and couldn't help noticing that the local hits became a bit bigger whenever they invited their fiancées to contribute backing vocals. After a minor hit in Japan with the English-language 'She's My Kind Of Girl', Björn and Benny felt sufficiently encouraged to record more English pop songs to which Frida and Agnetha were asked to contribute. Finally, on the 1972 song 'People Need Love', the girls shared the lead vocals equally with the men, and the result was the very first Abba single, although the quartet was credited as Björn & Benny, Agnetha & Anni-Frid.

Thus it was that six years after Björn and Benny first started working together they and their romantic partners finally decided to become permanent members of a group with the acronym-inspired name of Abba, which would be managed by Stig Anderson. Even so, it wasn't until the end of 1975, 18 months after their breakthrough with 'Waterloo', that the group finally became the musical priority for the individual members.

'Waterloo' alerted the world at large to Abba, winning the 1974 Eurovision song contest, held that year in Brighton. In many respects, winning Eurovision was a poisoned chalice, since few hitherto unknown winners from continental Europe had enjoyed anything like sustained international careers in music. However, the song contained many elements that lifted it beyond the typical Eurovision winner – it was a full-tilt rocker, delivered in the style of classic girl-group pop and produced with a nod to Phil Spector's magnificent Wall of Sound – and anyone with ears could tell that this group of Swedes had it in them to survive Eurovision's reputation for creating one-hit wonders and consigning them to oblivion.

In the event global success was almost two years away, partly because it took them a while to overcome the stigma of Eurovision but also because Abba had decided not to rush things, but to work painstakingly on their songs and sound in the studio with engineer Michael Tretow until they were 100% satisfied with the result. In the long term this far-sighted strategy, this scrupulous attention to quality control, was as responsible as anything in ensuring that several decades after it was recorded Abba's music would remain as popular as it does.

'Waterloo' reached number one in the UK charts and several other European countries in April 1974 but Abba had to wait until September of the following year before 'S.O.S' became their next big hit. In doing so it opened the floodgates. Between January 1976 and December 1981, the group enjoyed 16 top five hits in the UK alone, including eight number ones, all but one of which are included on *Abba Gold*. It was a chart run of dazzling proportions that in terms of quality and consistency over a similar period remains virtually unmatched.

As is the case with all groups that enjoy such spectacular success, all four members of Abba contributed crucial elements to the whole. Björn Ulvaeus was a natural leader and pragmatic decision maker, and also a keen lyricist, while Benny Andersson was a naturally gifted composer of pop melodies, schooled on the accordion as a child by his father and grandfather. Anni-Frid Lyngstad was a superb mid-range singer who brought a wealth of experience, both musical and personal, to bear in her interpretations. Blonde Agnetha Fältskog's higher register was crystal clear and, although she was perceived as the group's sex symbol, she often sang her leads with an air of wistful pathos that found empathy with women everywhere. This trace of melancholy that permeates much of Abba's work, even in songs that appear on the surface to be quite cheerful, is among their most distinctive – and unique – traits.

Just as it does today, Abba's music transcended fashion at the time it was released. In the UK and Europe punk was all the rage during Abba's glory years while in America new wave and disco were battling it out with mainstream rock delivered by men with beards in faded jeans and check shirts. The bright, often garish, clothing that Abba chose to wear was idiosyncratic to say the least, while their romantic pop, based largely on European melodic traditions, seemed out of phase with the times, though towards the end of their career they did produce some fine disco workouts.

Reluctant to tour until it proved impossible to refuse, Abba became pioneers of the video boom, astutely realising that producing short films of themselves singing their hits for distribution everywhere would preclude the need to perform hundreds of live shows throughout the world. In the end, of course, they succumbed, with predictable results – ticket riots, administrative chaos and general feelings of discontent and homesickness that placed an insurmountable strain on the relationships that held the group together.

Nevertheless, Abba's fame was truly international. Shrewdly, they recorded several of their songs in Spanish and German as well as their native Swedish. 'Dancing Queen' was a US number one. In Australia their popularity

was, and remains, second only to The Beatles. Huge crowds gathered at airports and outside hotels wherever they went on their memorable 1977 tour 'down under'. Famously, that same year London's Royal Albert Hall received a reported 3.5 million applications for a total of 12,000 tickets available for two concerts.

The group survived the breakdown of Björn's marriage to Agnetha and, since Björn was the group's lyricist, it is generally assumed that Abba's more heart-rending songs, tracks like 'Knowing Me, Knowing You', 'One Of Us' and the peerless 'The Winner Takes It All', were written from personal experience. Somehow, the shifting relationships within the group added another, distinctly poignant, string to their bow. By the time they last appeared together in December 1982, Benny's marriage to Frida was also over.

Abba had run its course. Björn and Benny wanted to write musicals together; Frida, the only member of the group who enjoyed live work, wanted a solo career; and Agnetha wanted nothing more than to be left alone to raise her children. But the music remained, heard at parties, at nostalgia festivals and, most notably, in discos frequented by the world's gay communities. There emerged a plethora of tribute bands, memorably led by an Australian outfit called Björn Again whose shows became instant sell-outs. Pete Waterman of the '80s chart-ruling team of Stock/Aitken/Waterman, singled out Lennon & McCartney, The Beach Boys, Motown and Abba as the ultimate role models for anyone who wanted to make hits, and when Waterman created the boy/girl group Steps in the late '90s his homage to Abba was never more overt.

By now many of the hippest stars from the next generation – U2, R.E.M., even Nirvana's Kurt Cobain – had all endorsed Abba. The icing on the cake was *Mamma Mia!*, the musical based on their songs which, having now been seen by over 30 million theatre-goers worldwide, has become the most successful musical of all time. The movie version, directed by the musical's original director, Phyllida Lloyd, and starring Meryl Streep and Pierce Brosnan, received its world premiere in June 2008.

The ongoing success of everything that Abba bequeathed to the world, the *Gold* album of songs that have become standards, the musical, the film, the tribute bands, and the pleasure they bring, is a triumph not just for the group or even its individual members. It is proof positive that the world's greatest popular music, as is contained within these pages, remains and will forever remain universally loved by succeeding generations for as long as our planet survives, truly a golden legacy.

Chris Charlesworth, October 2008
(With thanks to Carl Magnus Palm)

Dancing Queen

Words & Music by Benny Andersson,
Stig Anderson & Björn Ulvaeus

Moderate rock feel ♩ = 100

Knowing Me, Knowing You

Words & Music by Benny Andersson,
Stig Anderson & Björn Ulvaeus

Take A Chance On Me

Words & Music by Benny Andersson & Björn Ulvaeus

Moderately ♩ = 118

© Copyright 1977 Union Songs AB, Sweden.
Bocu Music Limited for Great Britain and the Republic of Ireland.
All rights in Germany administered by Universal Music Publ. GmbH.
All Rights Reserved. International Copyright Secured.

Mamma Mia

Words & Music by Benny Andersson,
Stig Anderson & Björn Ulvaeus

Lay All Your Love On Me

Words & Music by Benny Andersson & Björn Ulvaeus

With drive ♩ = 128

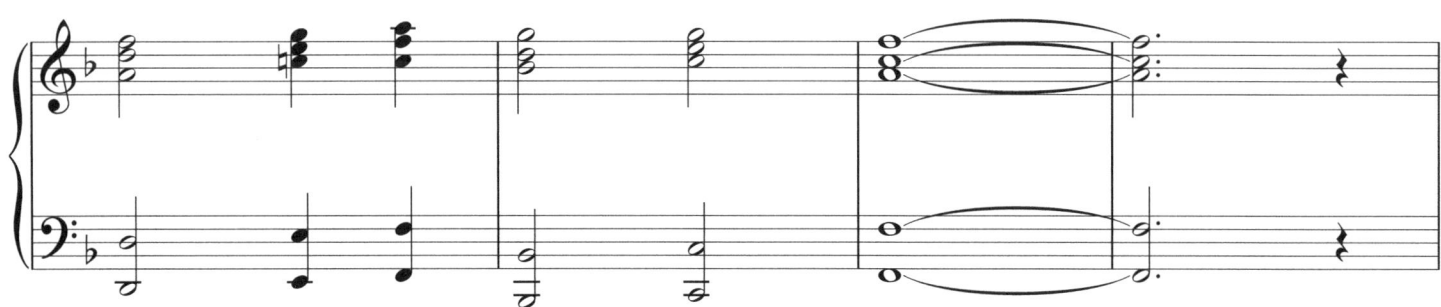

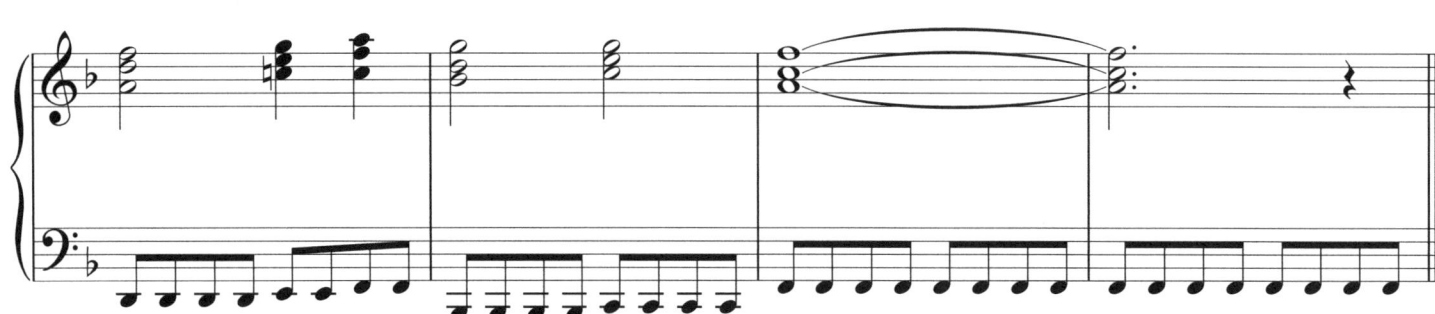

© Copyright 1980 Union Songs AB, Sweden.
Bocu Music Limited for Great Britain and the Republic of Ireland.
All rights in Germany administered by Universal Music Publ. GmbH.
All Rights Reserved. International Copyright Secured.

Super Trouper

Words & Music by Benny Andersson & Björn Ulvaeus

I Have A Dream

Words & Music by Benny Andersson & Björn Ulvaeus

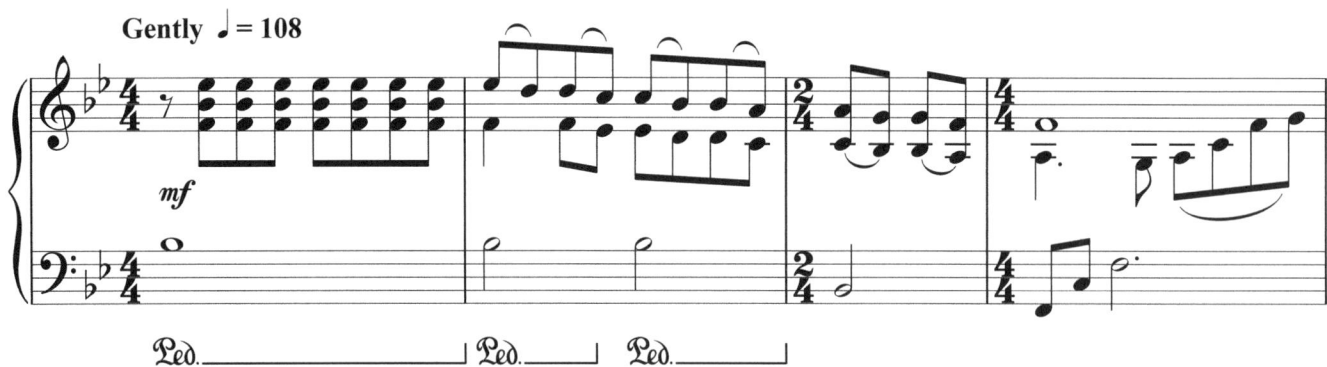

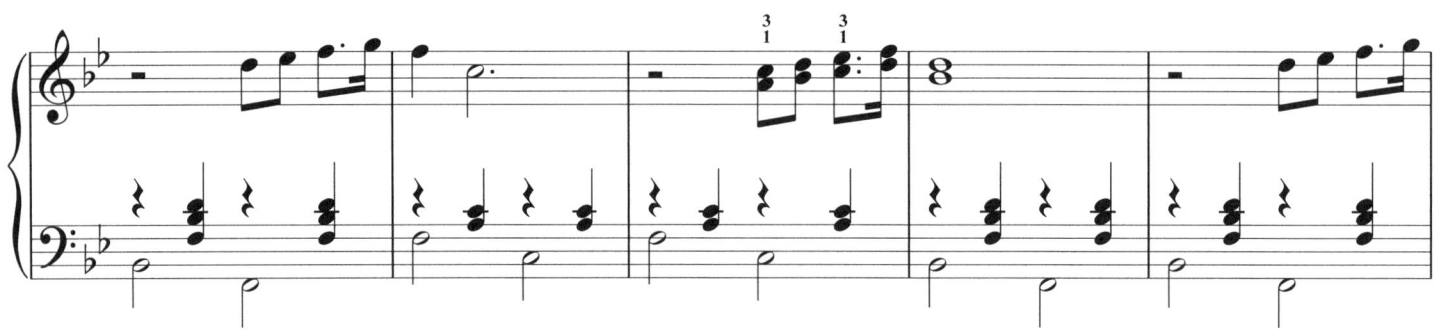

The Winner Takes It All

Words & Music by Benny Andersson & Björn Ulvaeus

Money, Money, Money

Words & Music by Benny Andersson & Björn Ulvaeus

S.O.S.

Words & Music by Benny Andersson,
Stig Anderson & Björn Ulvaeus

© Copyright 1975 Union Songs AB, Sweden.
Bocu Music Limited for Great Britain and the Republic of Ireland.
All rights in Germany administered by Universal Music Publ. GmbH.
All Rights Reserved. International Copyright Secured.

Chiquitita

Words & Music by Benny Andersson & Björn Ulvaeus

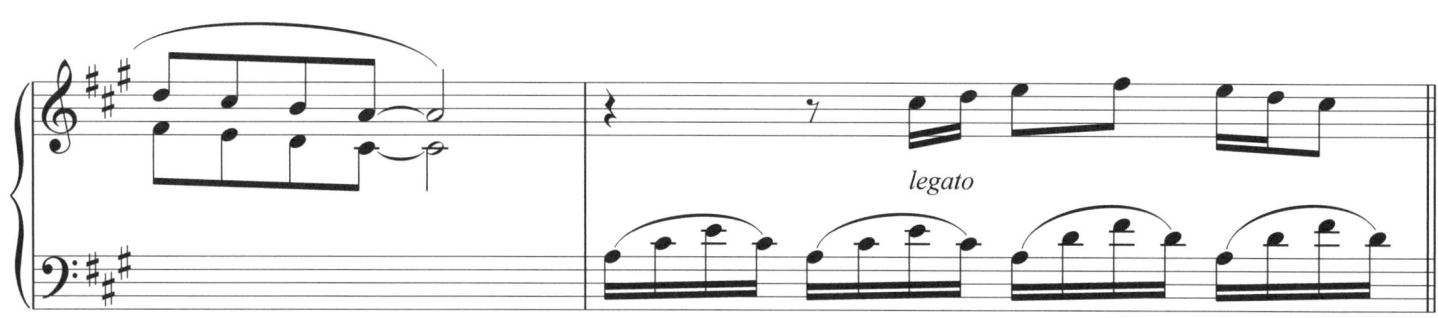
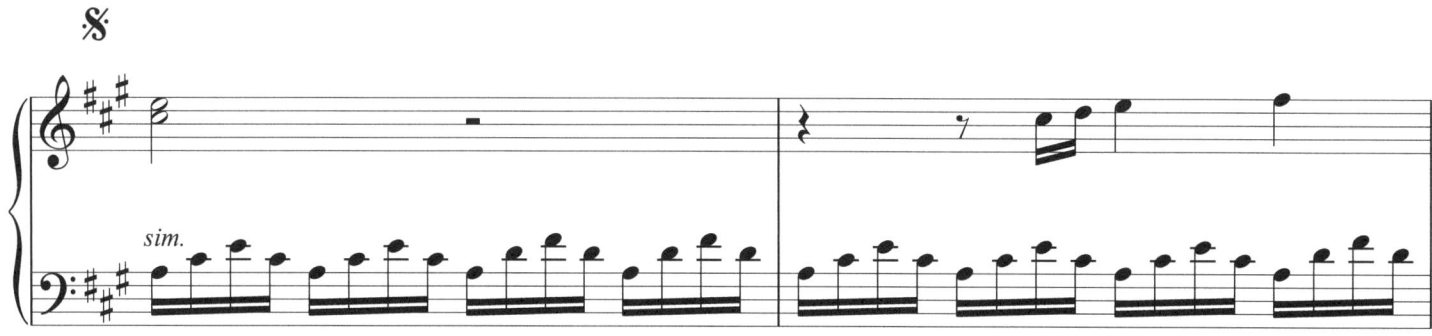

© Copyright 1979 Bocu Music Limited/Music for UNICEF.
All Rights Reserved. International Copyright Secured.

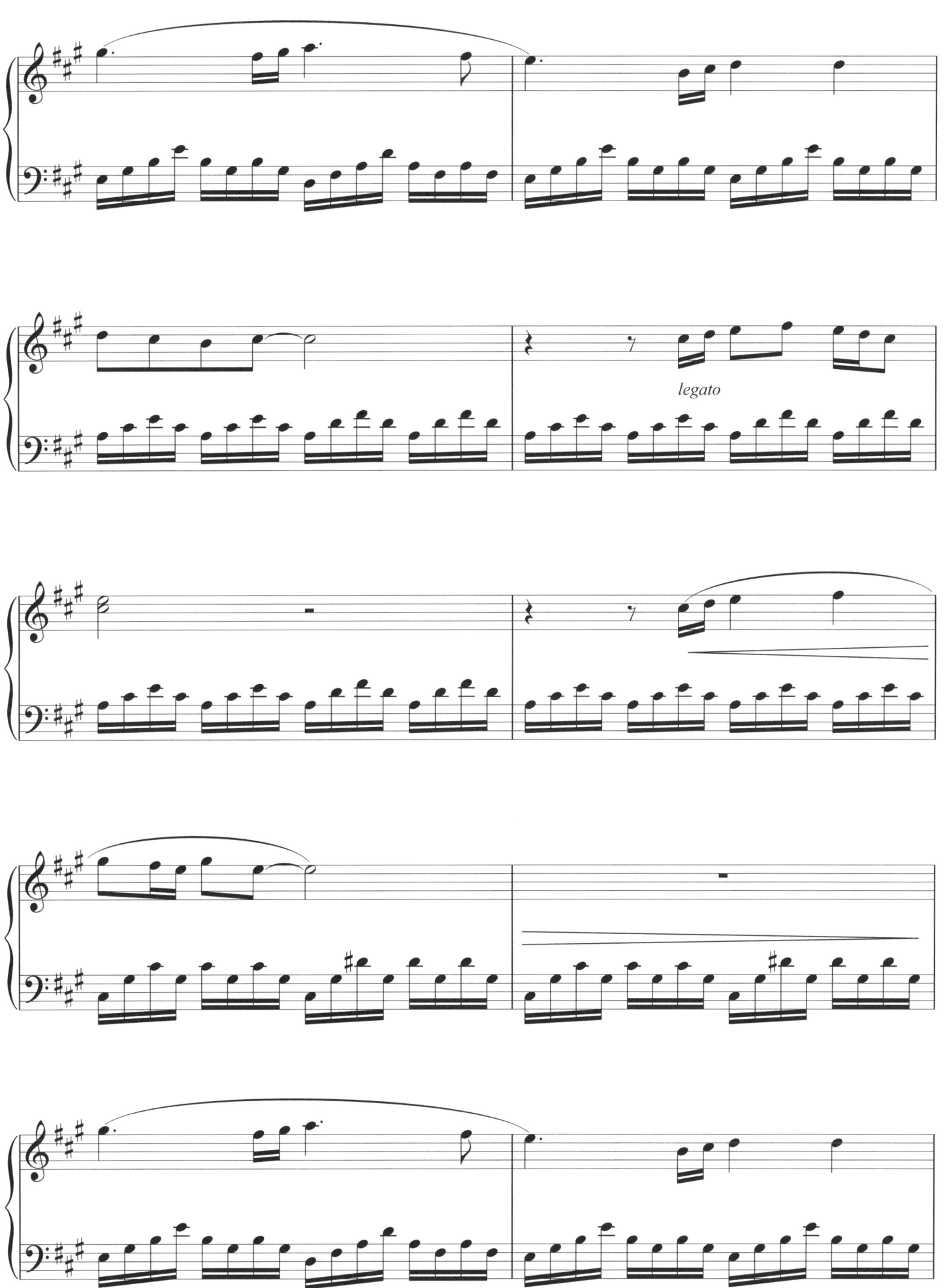

Fernando

Words & Music by Benny Andersson,
Stig Anderson & Björn Ulvaeus

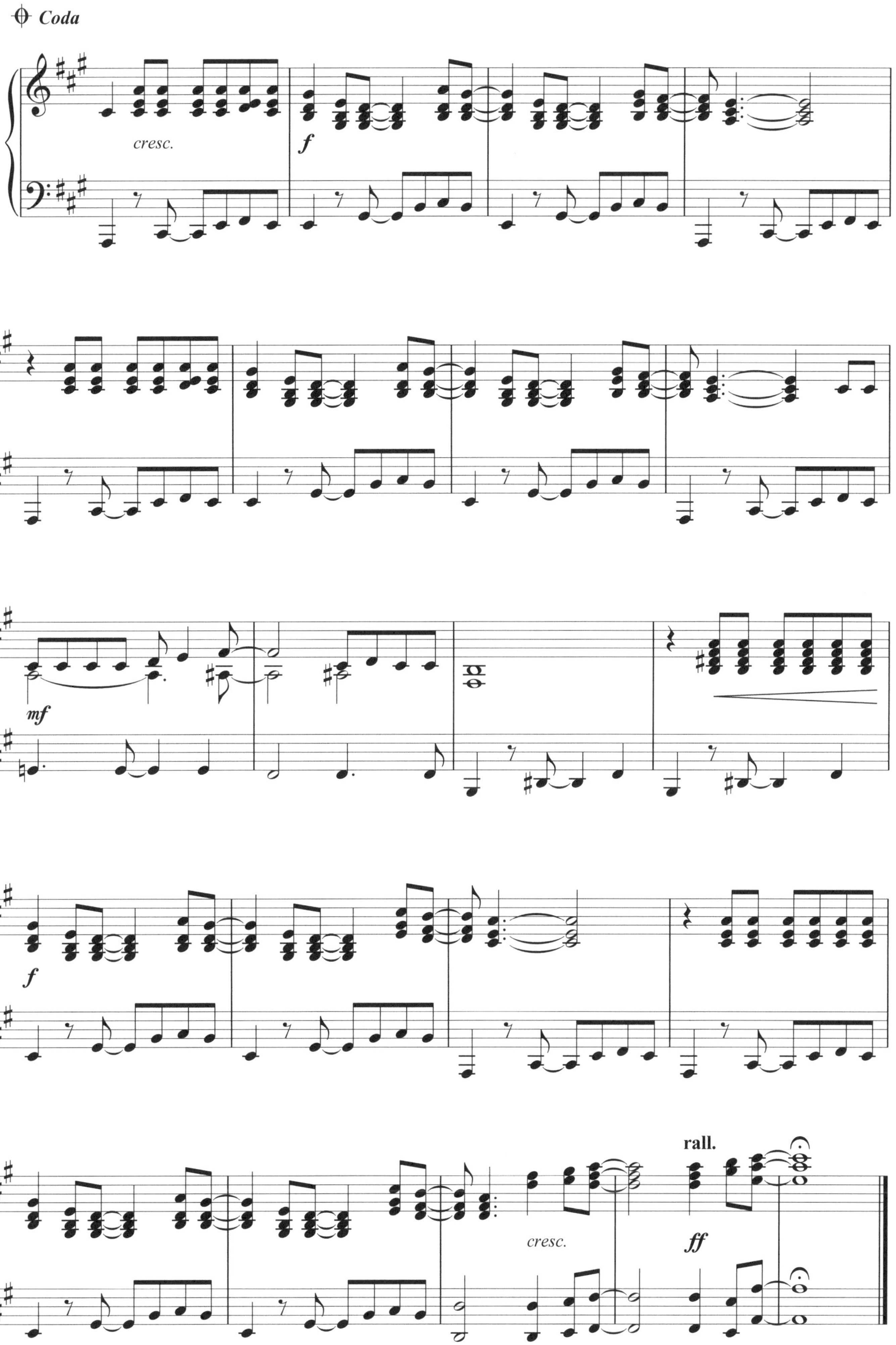
Coda
cresc.
f
mf
f
rall.
cresc.
ff

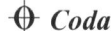

Gimme! Gimme! Gimme!
(A Man After Midnight)

Words & Music by Benny Andersson & Björn Ulvaeus

Does Your Mother Know

Words & Music by Benny Andersson & Björn Ulvaeus

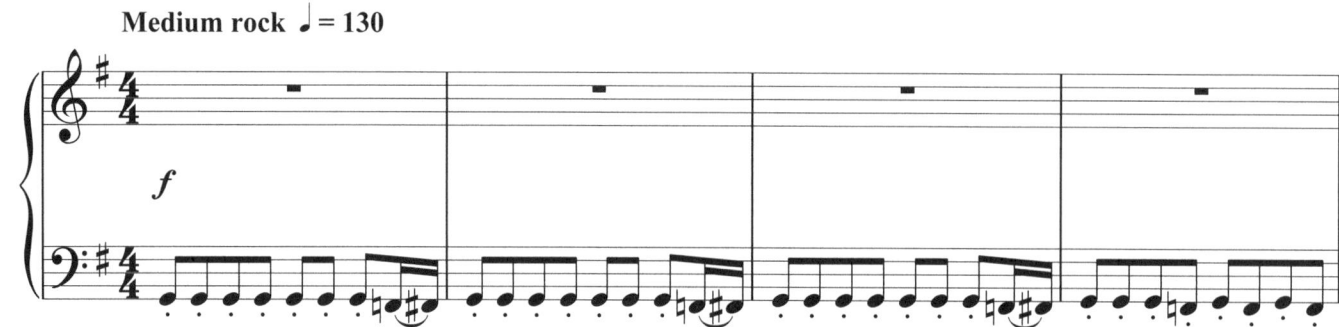

© Copyright 1979 Union Songs AB, Sweden.
Bocu Music Limited for Great Britain and the Republic of Ireland.
All rights in Germany administered by Universal Music Publ. GmbH.
All Rights Reserved. International Copyright Secured.

One Of Us

Words & Music by Benny Andersson & Björn Ulvaeus

© Copyright 1981 Union Songs AB, Sweden.
Bocu Music Limited for Great Britain and the Republic of Ireland.
All rights in Germany administered by Universal Music Publ. GmbH.
All Rights Reserved. International Copyright Secured.

The Name Of The Game

Words & Music by Benny Andersson,
Stig Anderson & Björn Ulvaeus

Thank You For The Music

Words & Music by Benny Andersson & Björn Ulvaeus

Waterloo

Words & Music by Benny Andersson,
Stig Anderson & Björn Ulvaeus

Bright shuffle ♩ = 142

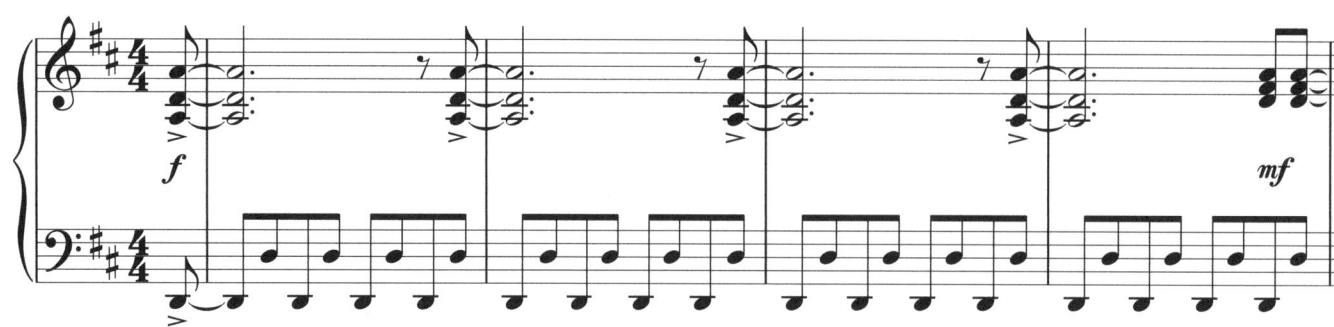

© Copyright 1974 Union Songs AB, Sweden.
Bocu Music Limited for Great Britain and the Republic of Ireland.
All rights in Germany administered by Universal Music Publ. GmbH.
All Rights Reserved. International Copyright Secured.

Voulez-Vous

Words & Music by Benny Andersson & Björn Ulvaeus